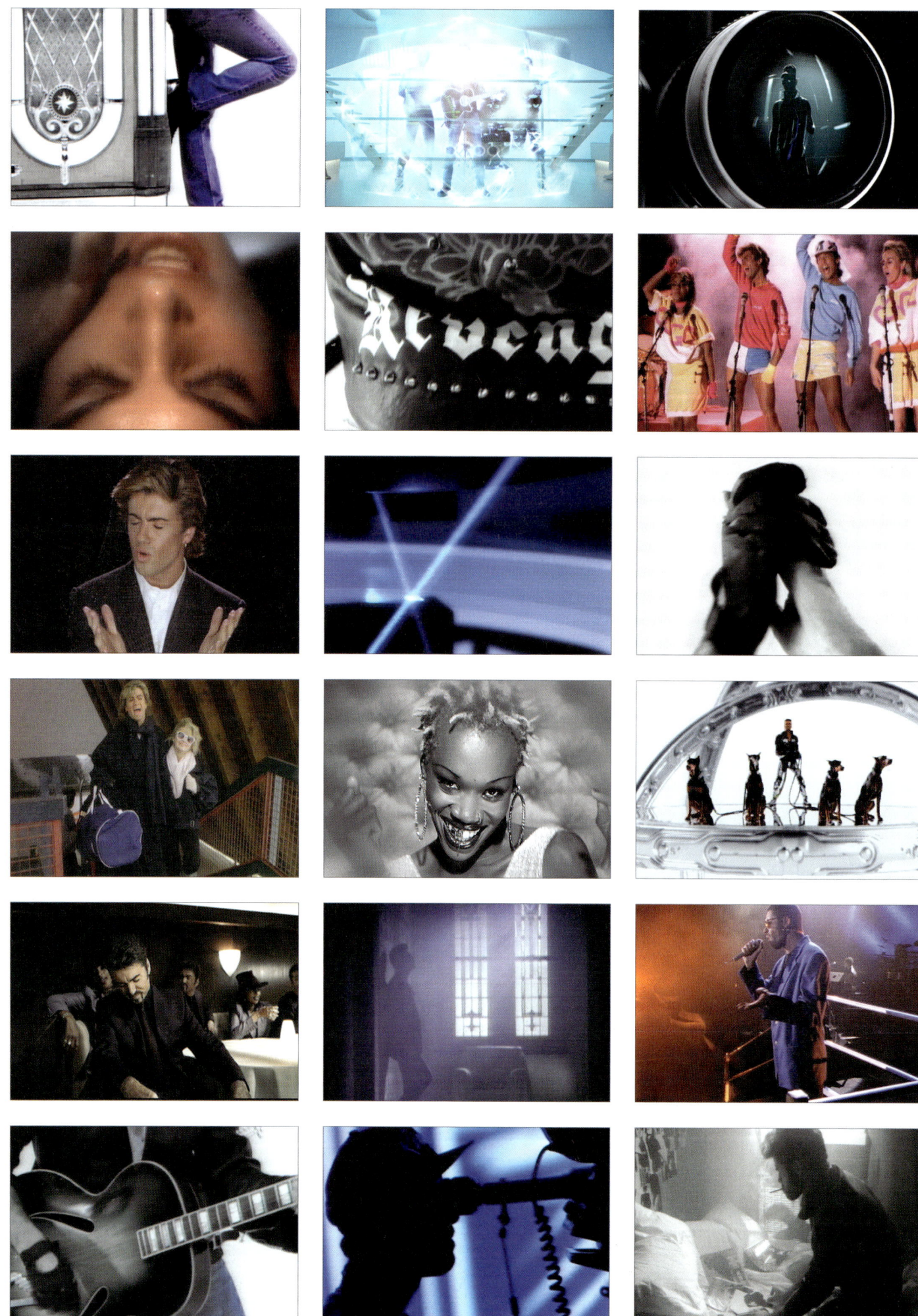

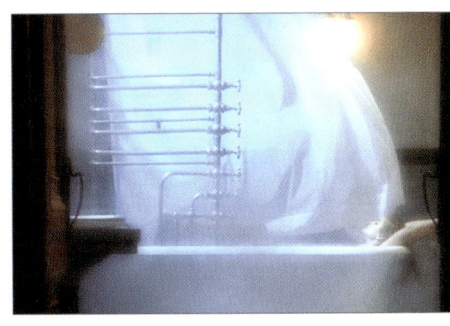

FOR THE LOYAL

6	UNDERSTAND
11	PRECIOUS BOX
21	ROXANNE
26	FANTASY
35	CARS AND TRAINS
44	PATIENCE
48	YOU KNOW THAT I WANT TO
52	MY MOTHER HAD A BROTHER
60	IF YOU WERE THERE
64	SAFE
69	AMERICAN ANGEL
76	MY BABY JUST CARES FOR ME
80	BROTHER CAN YOU SPARE A DIME?
86	PLEASE SEND ME SOMEONE
96	THROUGH

© 2007 by Faber Music Ltd
First published by Faber Music Ltd in 2007
3 Queen Square, London WC1N 3AU

Re-Engravings : Cotswold Music Typesetting.
New Arrangements : Richard Harris.
Editor : Lucy Holliday.
Cover Design : George Michael and Simon Halfon.
Cover Photography : Andrew Macpherson.

Printed in England by Caligraving Ltd.
All Rights Reserved.

The text paper used in this publication is a virgin fibre product
that is manufactured in the UK to ISO 14001 standards.
The wood fibre used is only sourced from managed forests using
sustainable forestry principles. This paper is 100% recyclable

ISBN10: 0-571-52996-8
EAN13: 978-0-571-52996-4

To buy Faber Music publications or to find out about the full range of titles available,
please contact your local music retailer or Faber Music sales enquiries :

Faber Music Ltd, Burnt Mill, Elizabeth Way,
Harlow, CM20 2HX England.
tel:+44(0)1279 82 89 82 fax:+44(0)1279 82 89 83
sales@fabermusic.com fabermusic.com

PRECIOUS BOX

Words and Music by George Michael

© 2003 Aegean Music
Warner/Chappell Music Ltd, London W6 8BS

ROXANNE

Words and Music by Gordon Sumner

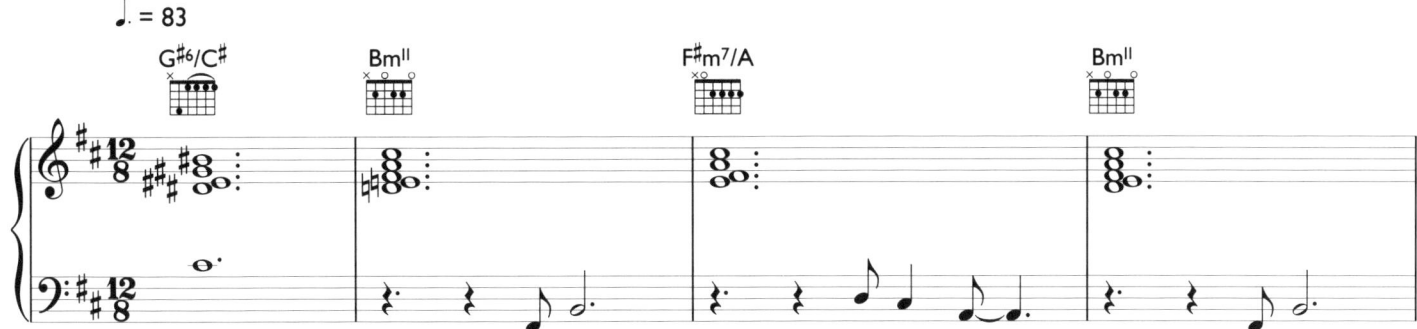
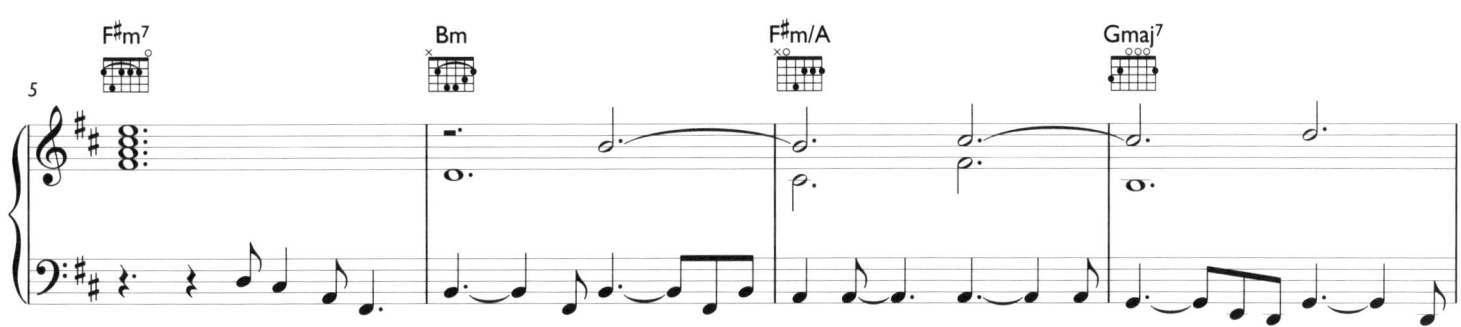

© 1978 GM Sumner
EMI Music Publishing Ltd, London WC2H 0QY (Publishing) and
Music Sales Ltd, London W1T 3LJ (Print)

FANTASY

Words and Music by George Michael

CARS AND TRAINS

Words and Music by Jonathan Douglas and George Michael

© 2003 Warner/Chappell Music Ltd and Aegean Music
Warner/Chappell Music Ltd, London W6 8BS

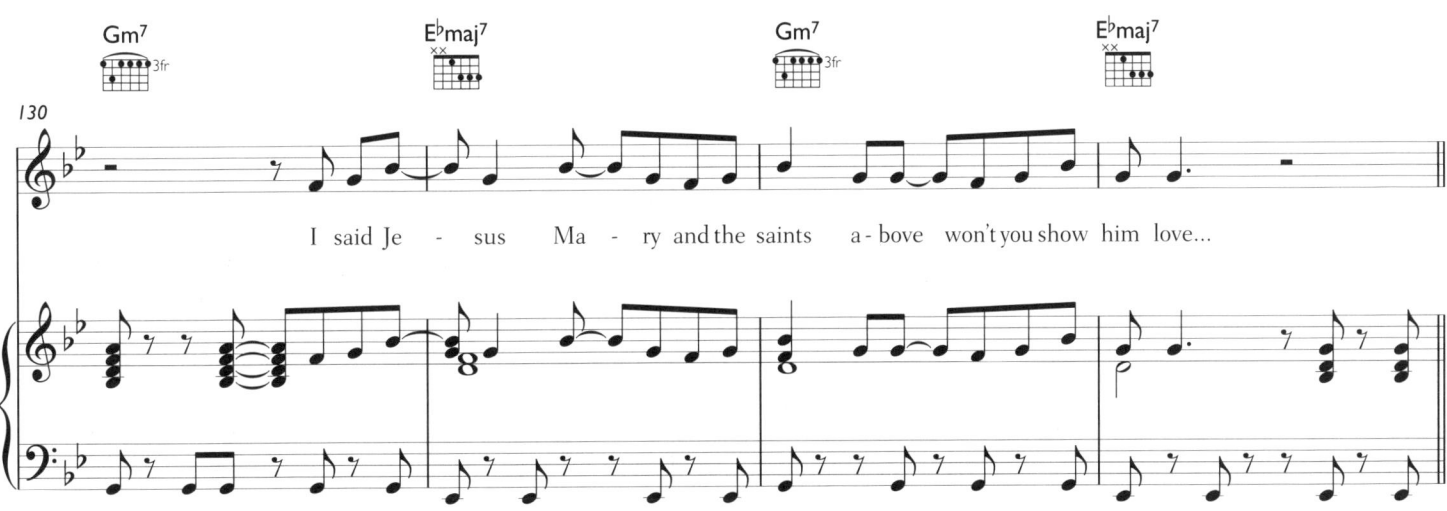

PATIENCE

Words and Music by George Michael

♩ = 60 **Freely**

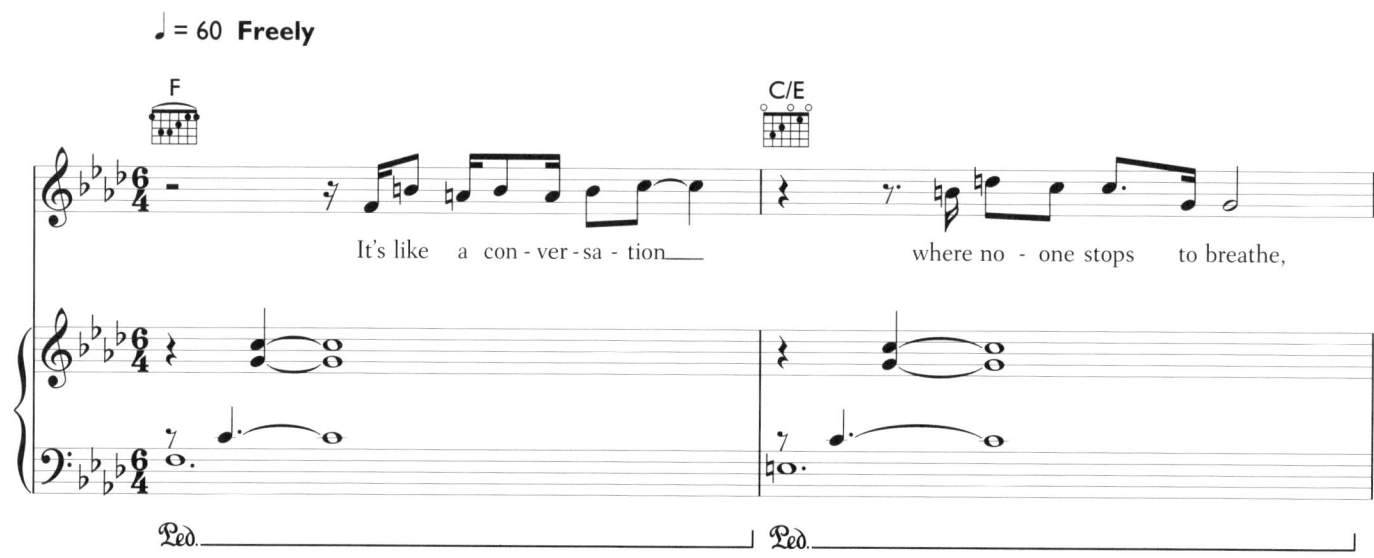

It's like a con-ver-sa-tion where no-one stops to breathe,

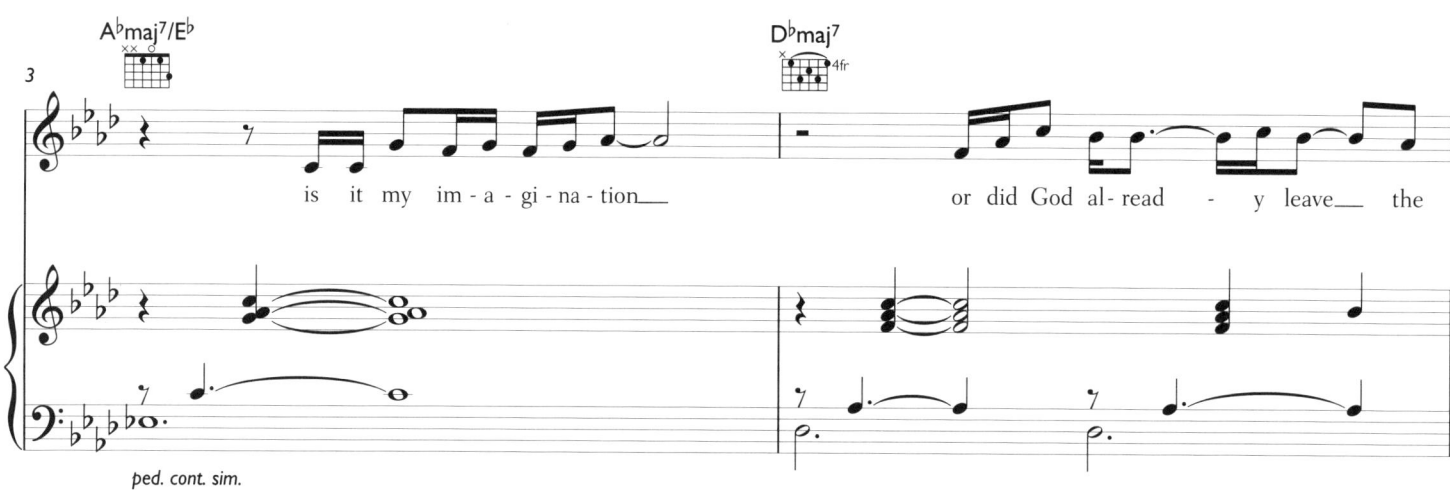

is it my im-a-gi-na-tion or did God al-read-y leave the

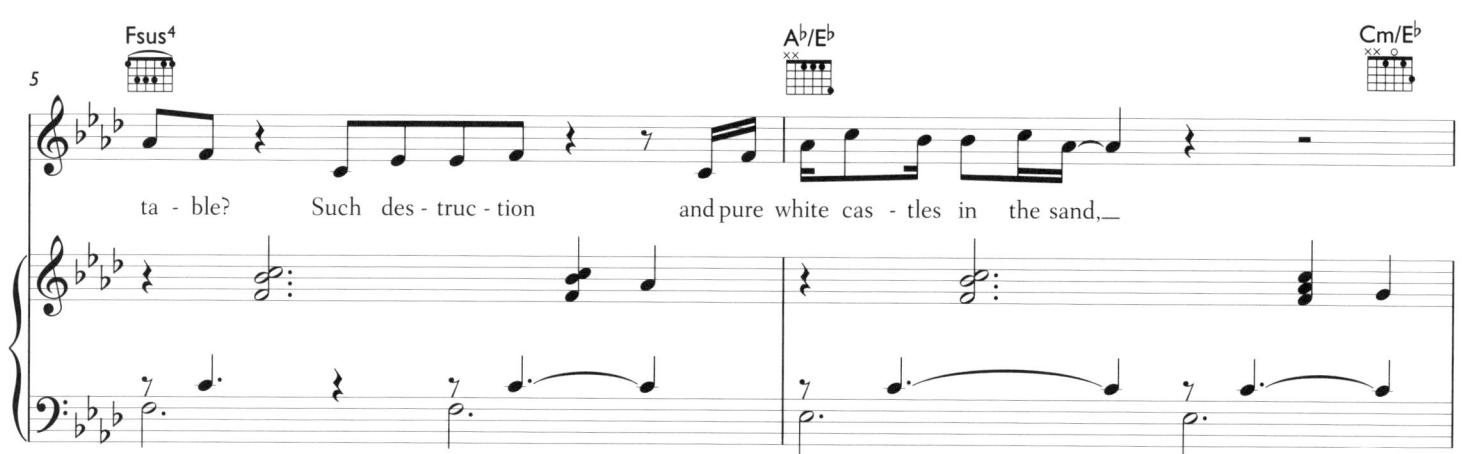

ta-ble? Such des-truc-tion and pure white cas-tles in the sand,

© 2004 Aegean Music
Warner/Chappell Music Ltd, London W6 8BS

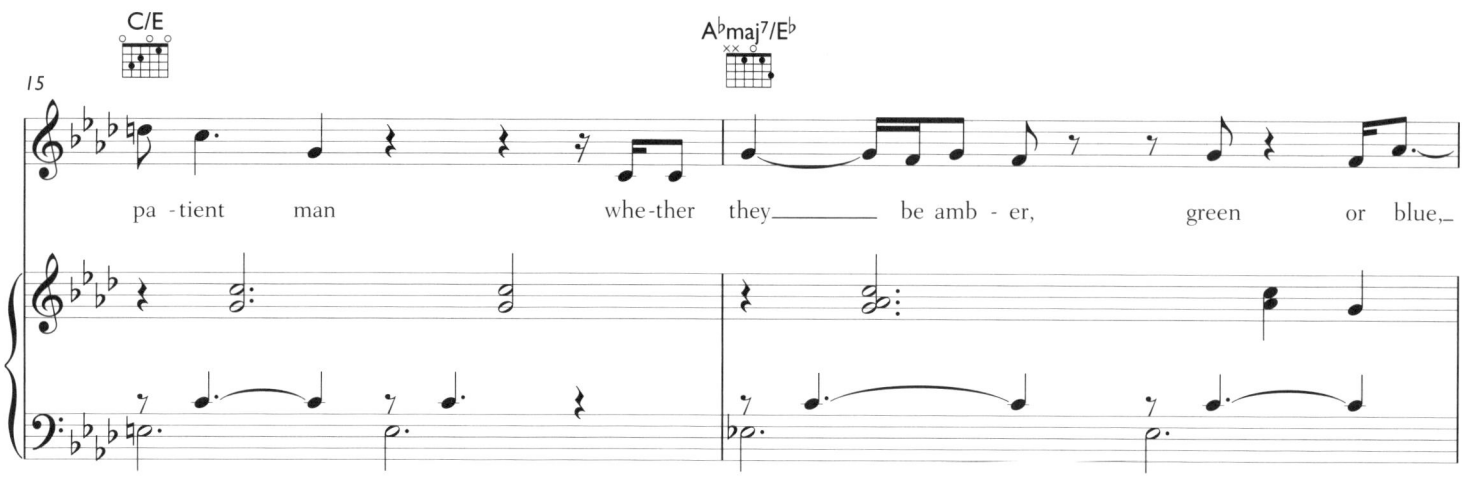

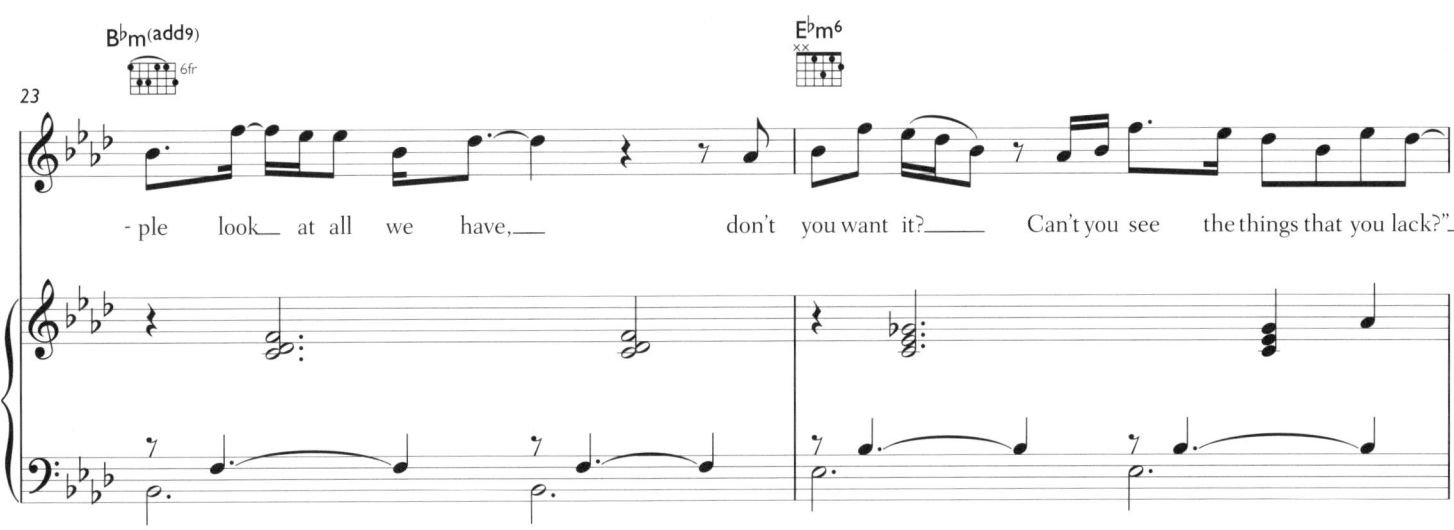

YOU KNOW THAT I WANT TO

Words and Music by George Michael and Johnny Douglas

© 1996 Robobuild Ltd and Rondor Music (London) Ltd
Warner/Chappell Music Ltd, London W6 8BS and
Rondor Music (London) Ltd, London SW6 4LZ

MY MOTHER HAD A BROTHER

Words and Music by George Michael

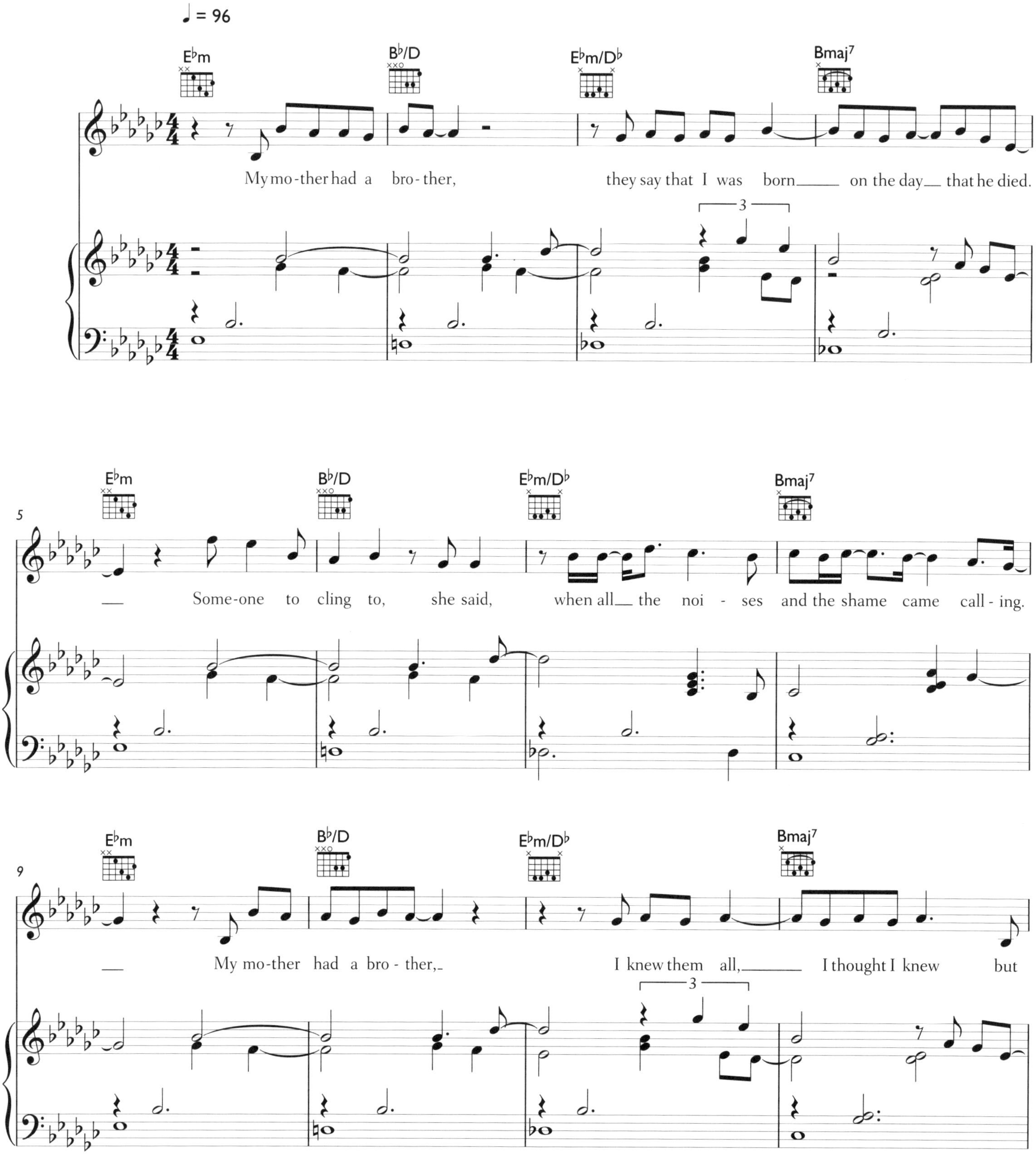

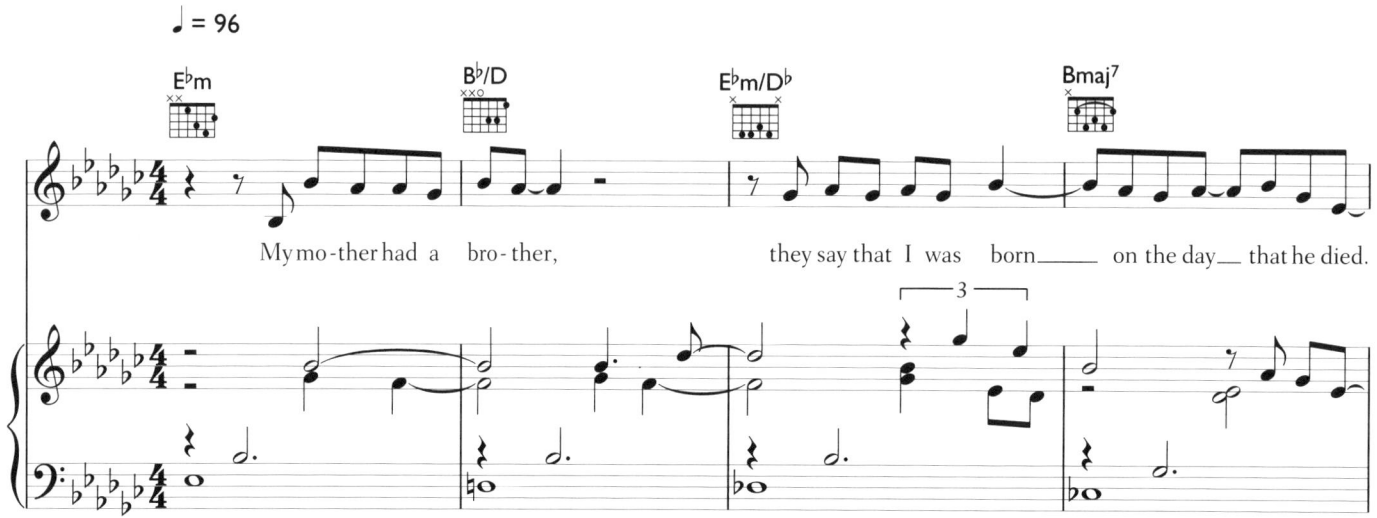

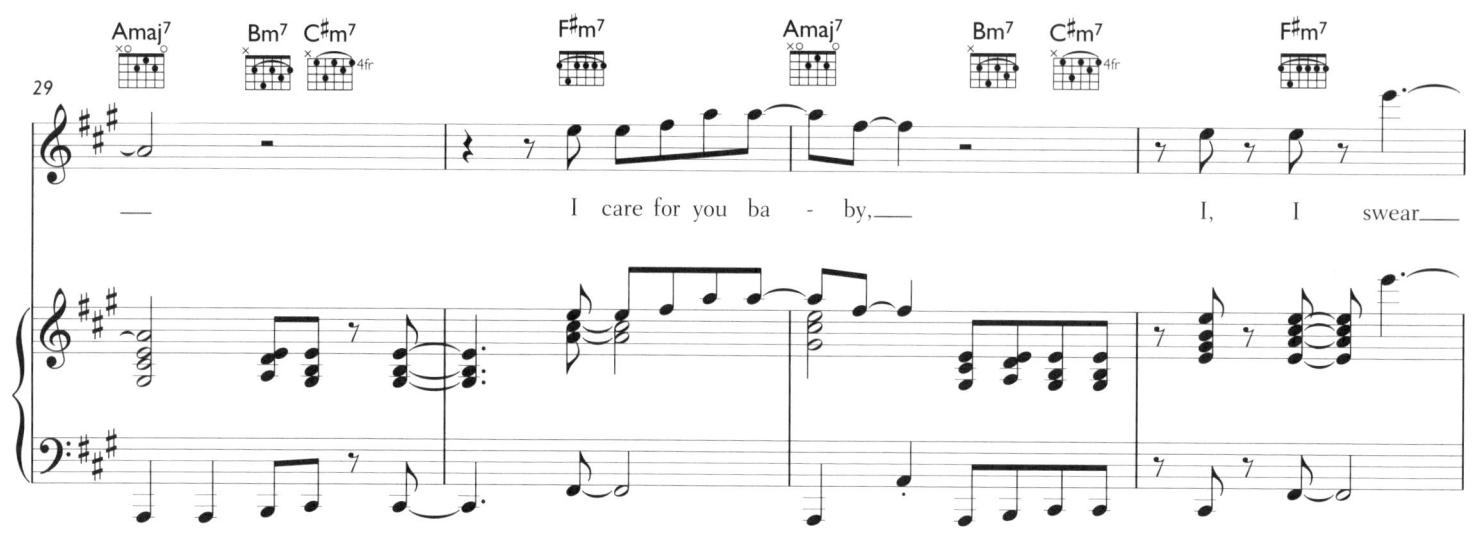
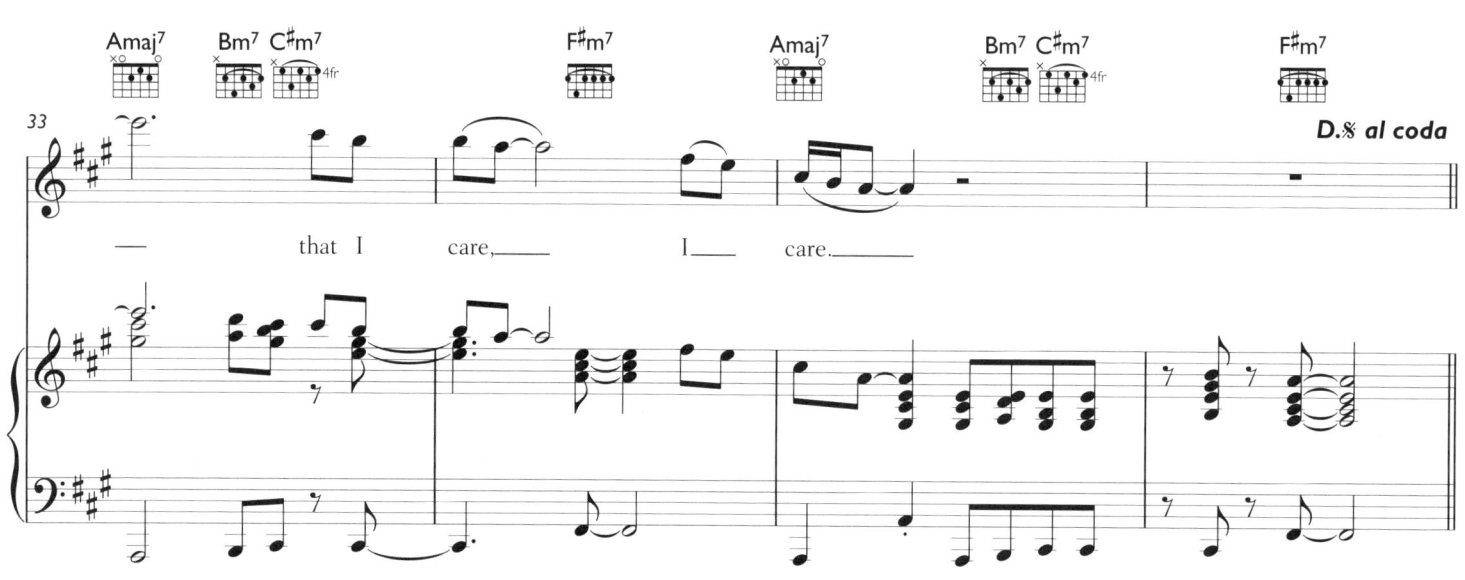

SAFE

Words and Music by George Michael

© 1996 Robobuild Ltd
Warner/Chappell Music Ltd, London W6 8BS

MY BABY JUST CARES FOR ME

Words by Gus Kahn
Music by Walter Donaldson

© 1930 Bregman Vocco & Conn Inc, USA
EMI Music Publishing Ltd, London WC2H 0QY

BROTHER CAN YOU SPARE A DIME?

Words by E Y Harburg
Music by Jay Gorney

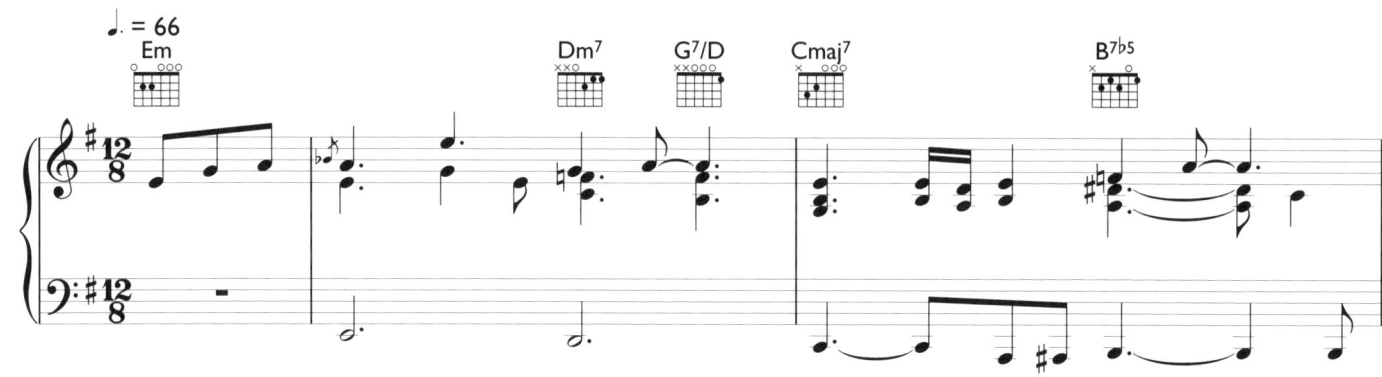
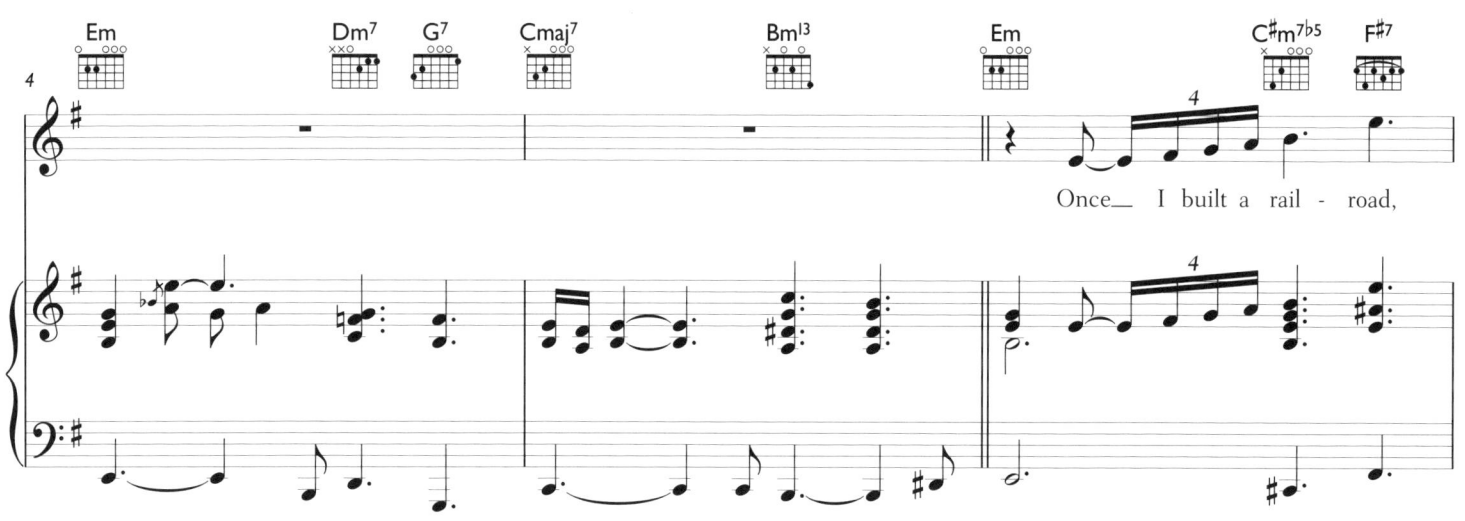
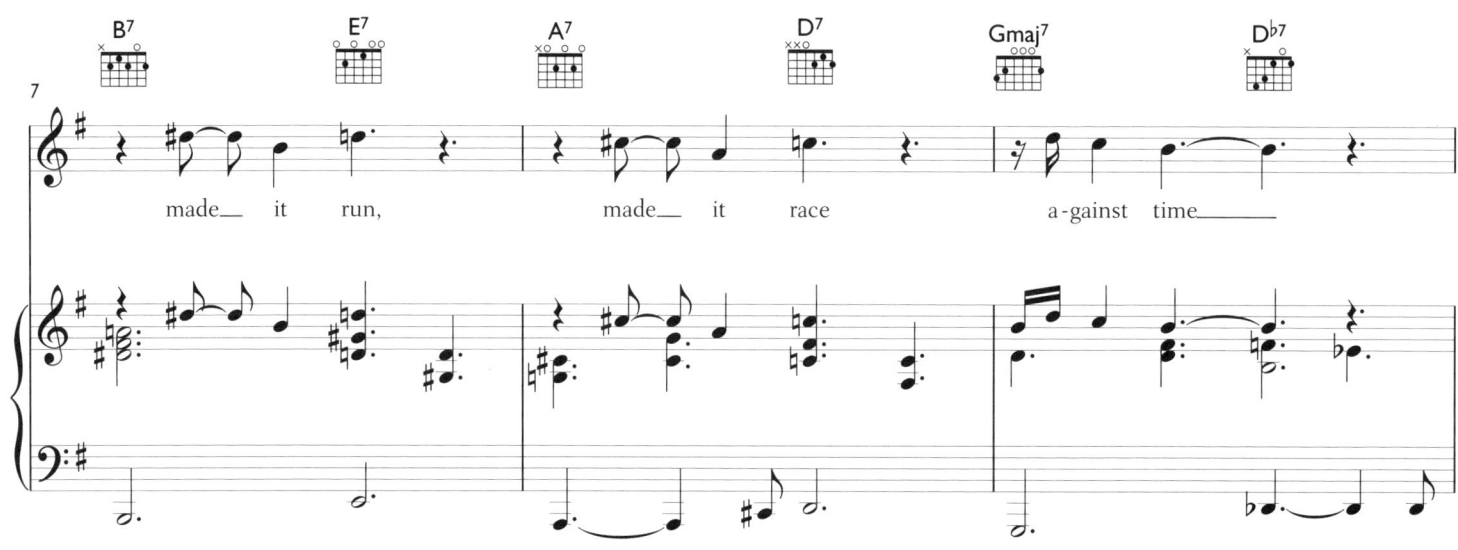

© 1932 Harms Inc and Glocca Morra Music Corp, USA
Warner/Chappell Music Ltd, London W6 8BS and
Carlin Music Corp, London NW1 8BD

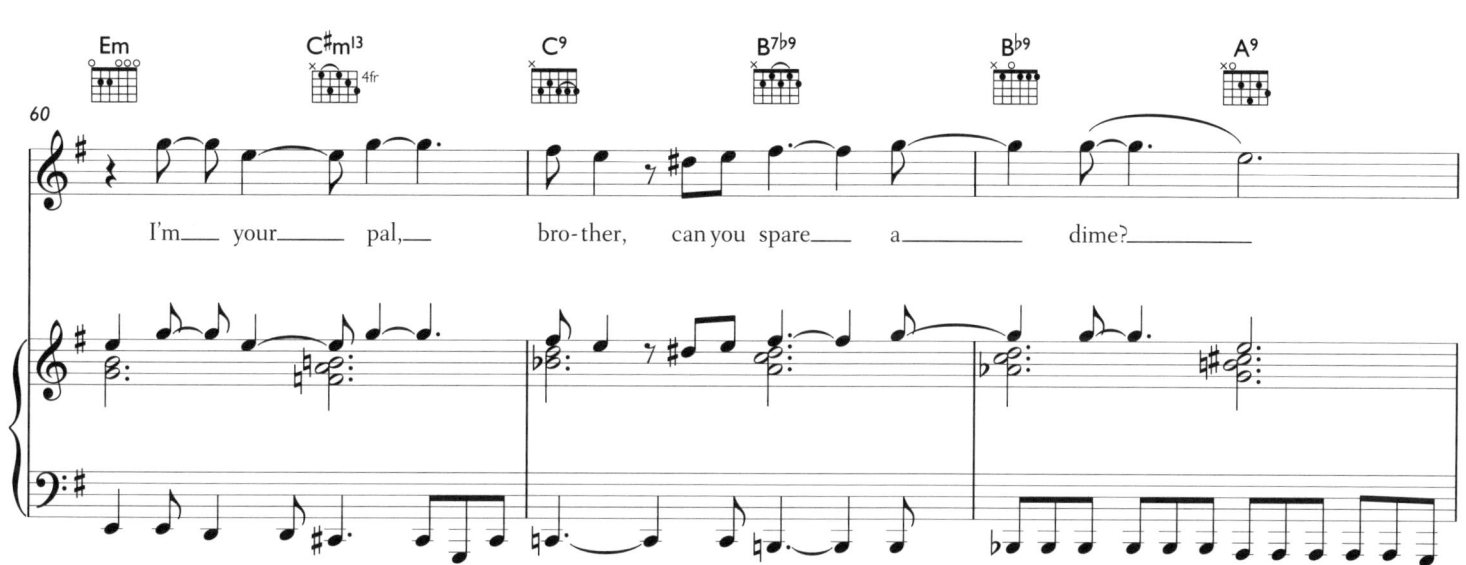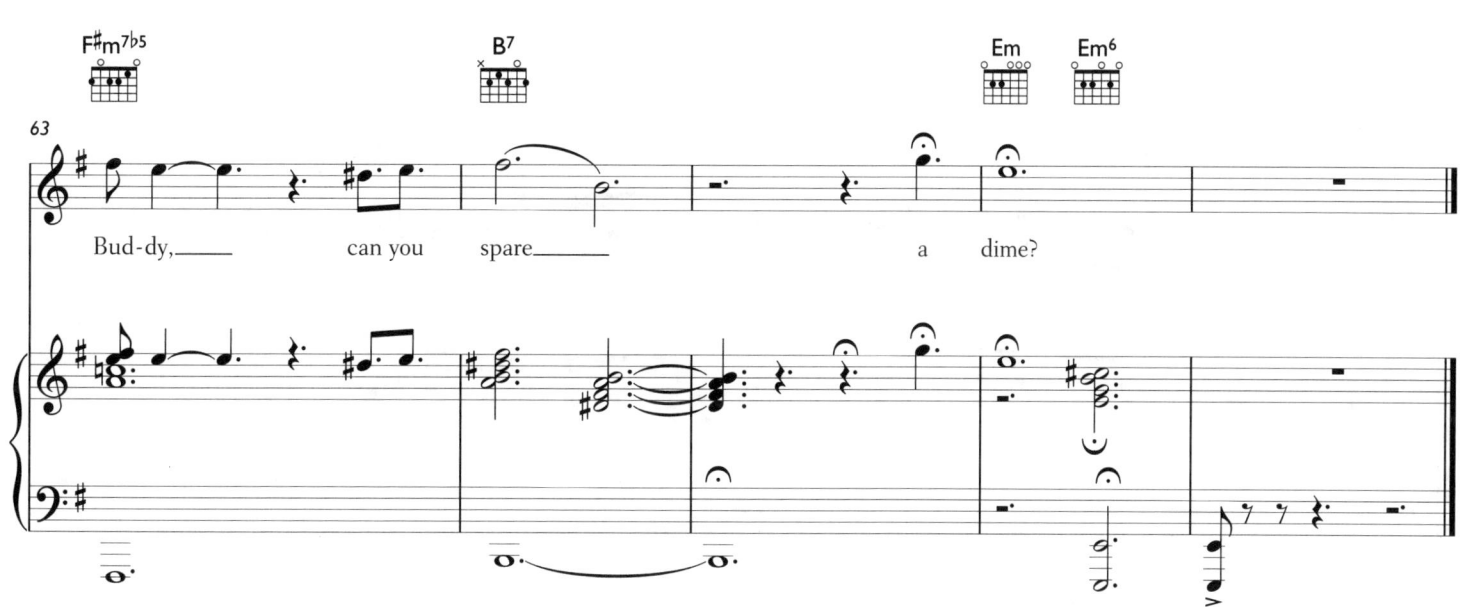

PLEASE SEND ME SOMEONE

Words by George Michael and Hal David
Music by George Michael and John Barry

original key F# major

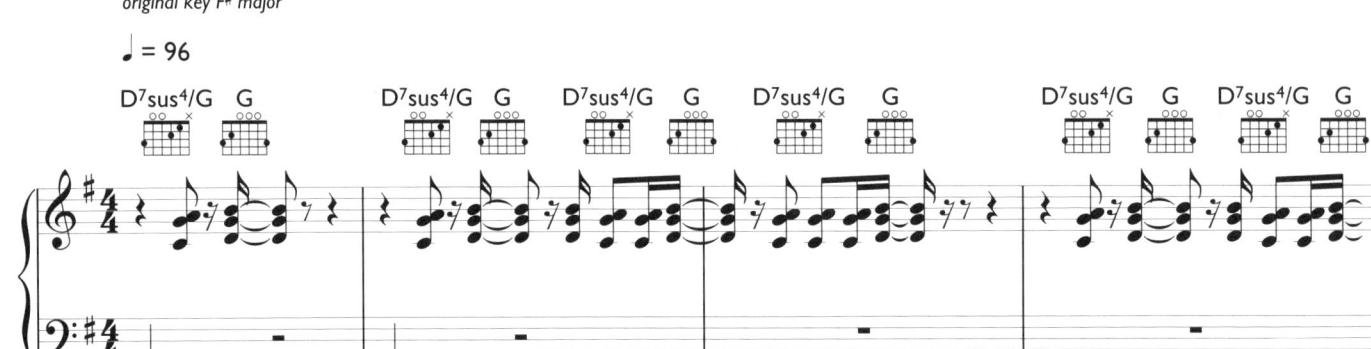

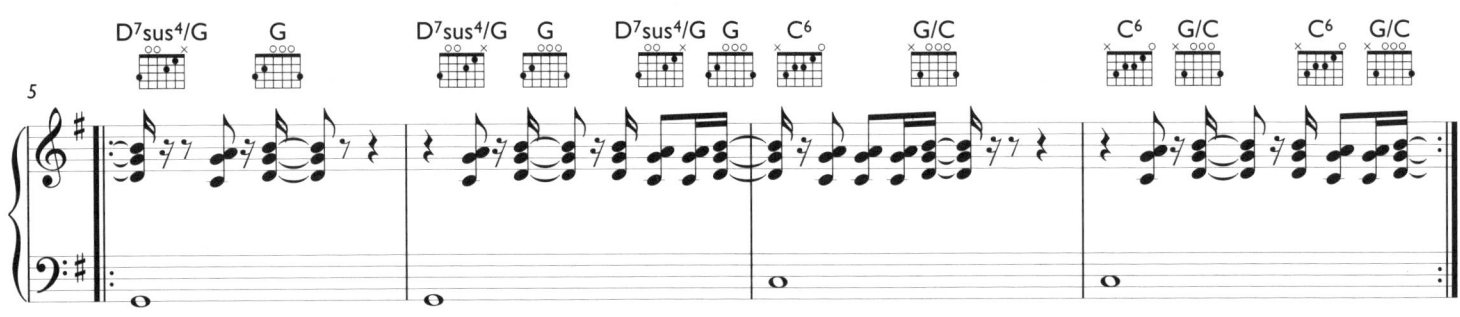

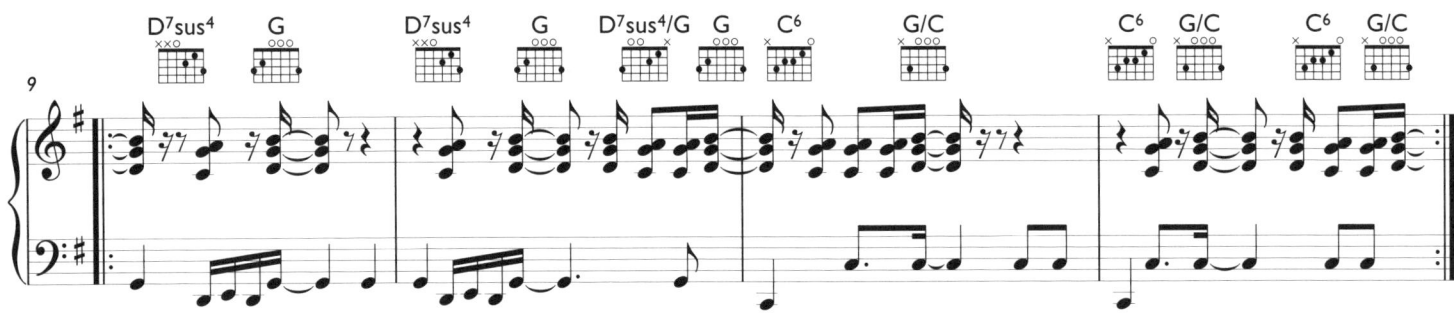

1. Some peo- ple say if I could on- ly care___ for you,

© 2003 Aegean Music and United Artists Music Co Inc, USA
Warner/Chappell Music Ltd, London W6 8BS and EMI United Partnership Ltd, London WC2H 0QY (Publishing) and Alfred Publishing Co, USA (Print)
Administered in Europe by Faber Music Ltd
[This song contains a sample from "Moonraker" by David & Barry © United Artists Music Co Inc, USA

THROUGH

Words and Music by George Michael

© 2003 Aegean Music
Warner/Chappell Music Ltd, London W6 8BS